JIU JITSU

TRAINING JOURNAL

JIU JITSU
TRAINING JOURNAL

BETHANY MARSHALL &
LEE BAUCOM

AITIA PRESS • NEW YORK

JIU JITSU
TRAINING JOURNAL

Published in New York, New York, by Aitia Press, a branded imprint of Morgan James Publishing. Morgan James is a trademark of Morgan James, LLC. www.aitiapress.com

ISBN 978-1-63195-042-1 paperback
ISBN 978-1-63195-043-8 eBook
Library of Congress Control Number: 2020902741

Cover Design by:
Chris Treccani
www.3dogcreative.net

Cover Photograph by:
Shamil Ramazonov taken at Masterskya
in downtown Brooklyn, New York.

Morgan James is a proud partner of Habitat for Humanity Peninsula
and Greater Williamsburg. Partners in building since 2006.

Get involved today! Visit
www.MorganJamesBuilds.com

INTRODUCTION

Welcome to your jiu jitsu journal! This can be an important tool in your jiu jitsu learning—and your life.

First, note that this is *your* journal. It will only become a useful resource when you claim it as your journal. Even if you aren't quite sure how to get the best use from it, start. How you use it will improve and change over time—but only if you use it!

Any tool is only as useful as it is used. You will find this to be true both about this journal and you. The more you learn in jiu jitsu, the more you will want it to be accessible and part of your muscle memory. Practice and lessons are important. The details of the lessons, though, can quickly fade in your mind. After all, life is busy.

This journal gives you a place to process and record what you are learning in class. Then, when you can't quite recall a detail, you will have a place to reference.

The creators of this journal are both practitioners. One of us is a longtime veteran of MMA and no-gi jiu jitsu, and the other is a fairly recent practitioner (two years of experience so far), so this journal was created by practitioners for practitioners. The journal is the tool we wish we had at the start of our learning. We have sought to create a tool you can use for your entire rolling life. From beginner to advanced practitioner, this journal will help you progress as efficiently and proficiently as possible. It is the tool we both would have loved at the start of our own journeys.

Before jumping into the journal, be sure and read through the rest of this opening section for tips on how to stay healthy and safe, how to be a great partner, how to roll for life, and how to be a great student at any stage. Then, jump in and use the journal!

Take it to class and get started. Just follow the simple directions later in the opening section. We hope this tool helps you find your jiu jitsu journey even more rewarding and powerful.

Let's get started! And keep on rolling!

GYM RULES

A jiu jitsu gym is a place unlike any other place. It can feel like a home away from home. A place where you are challenged physically, mentally, and emotionally. It's important that you care for your gym and help foster a supportive environment for your best learning and the benefit of everyone.

Here are some basic rules that will help everyone (including you) have a great experience while learning the art of jiu jitsu.

- Questions should always be welcomed, but **be mindful not to interrupt**. Students are encouraged to wait until the instructor has prompted for questions before asking them.
- **Allow the instructor to do the instructing**. If you think you have a better approach to a move that is being taught or another variation to share, ask the instructor after the teaching moment.
- **Avoid profanity.** Especially when young ears are around. Profanity isn't necessary and can be uncomfortable for others.
- Ensure you leave with all of your belongings at the end of practice and keep your things tidy while they are at the gym. **Clean up after yourself!**
- **Help keep the mats clean.** Regularly volunteer to help clean the mats after practice.

- Remember, while this sport may range from anything from a hobby to self-defense to serious competition for you, the owner of your facility has made an investment and many sacrifices to ensure its doors are open. **Be diligent with paying your tuition on time.** Support your gym so it can be there to support you.

HEALTHY ROLLING

Jiu jitsu is an active sport that will push your body. It is also a contact sport. You are constantly in extremely close proximity to your training partners, not to mention the mats. Healthy training will keep you on the mats.

A few basic, but important, tips can help make sure you don't have unnecessary, long gaps in training that could be prevented. These tips will help keep you (and others) healthy and safe.

- **Never wear your shoes on the mats**. You are up close and personal with the mats. So, anything that is on the bottom of your shoes will end up on the mats. Which will end up on you.
- **Always wear your shoes in the bathroom or whenever you are off the mats**. This will keep your bare feet clean for the mats.
- **Shower as soon as possible after training**. Don't wait hours and hours. Ringworm, impetigo, and other transferable skin infections can spread quickly on the mats. Showering quickly will help keep your skin clear of infections and ready to roll.
- **Keep your gi clean!** Wash it after every use. For both hygiene reasons and also as a courtesy to your teammates. A clean gi is free of potentially infectious organisms and makes partner work more pleasant.

- **If you have a skin infection, refrain from training until it is cleared up.** You will have to miss practice. But skin infections can spread quickly when in such close contact.
- **If you are sick, stay off the mats.** You will recover more quickly, and you will also protect others. While sharing is good, sharing germs is not!
- **Finger and toenails should be trimmed so you don't scratch your partner.** This will prevent cuts, which can lead to bleeding and open wounds. Even small wounds make easy entrances for infections.
- **Remove jewelry before class.** Jewelry can pose a threat to you, your partner, and the mats.
- **Treat any blood as a biohazard.** When you notice blood, stop and address it. Notify the instructor and find the source. And be sure to clean your gi of any blood when you get home.
- **Don't skip warming up!** Warm-ups are intended to help prime your body for the motions it will be doing and the positions it will be in over the course of your class.
- **Avoid OVERtraining (yes, there is such a thing).** Your body does need time to rest and recover to function at its best, as well as to defend itself from illness, infection, and injuries. Listen to your body.
- **If you are dealing with an injury, consult your doctor and modify your training according to their recommendation.** Many times, it is possible to continue practicing with minor injuries. But you can make a minor injury much worse when you don't attend to it early.
- **If you have gotten the okay to train with an injury, communicate with your partners so they are aware and can avoid making the injury worse.** Let your partner know what you can and cannot do. Then make sure you both follow those guidelines.
- When rolling, **remember never to be too proud to tap**. A quick tap today could be the thing that allows you to participate in training tomorrow.
- How you treat your body in your time off the mats is also important. **Healthy diet, sleep, and fitness choices are crucial to how your body and mind perform on the mats.**

Jiu jitsu is a unique sport, partly due to the close contact with others and with the mats. It is a great source of exercise and self-defense. Protecting yourself and your partners will let everyone enjoy the sport for as long as possible, as safely as possible. Do your part to protect yourself and others.

HOW TO BE A GREAT PARTNER

Your training partners are some of the most instrumental factors in the improvement of your jiu jitsu game. Your relationship with your partners will vary from individual to individual. Some will challenge, frustrate, or perhaps even anger you at times. Others will inspire, motivate, and push you to be your best. All types of partners are important to encounter as you seek to become a well-rounded practitioner of jiu jitsu.

As you work with various partners, you can learn something from everyone you work with. You'll also discover that there is an art to being a good partner, but becoming a good partner is not complicated. With focus in a few key areas, you'll quickly become a high-quality and trusted training partner.

- **Be encouraging, supportive, and respectful.** You and your partner are there to learn. Be supportive of your common goal and of each other.
- **Show up engaged and focused.** It's motivating to work with an engaged and enthusiastic partner. Don't "dilly dally" around. Lazy motions and movements can be off-putting and demotivating.
- **Communicate throughout practice with your partner.** If you can key your partner into how their move is working on you and indicate how their positioning and pressure is working, it will increase their ability to

accurately hit the move when rolling live, in competition or when needed in a self-defense situation.

- **Allow ample time for your partner to tap.** In other words, do not go from "0 to 100" when executing your move. In some positions or submissions, the difference between a safe place and point of injury can be an inch or less. Start slowly and methodically and build from there. Few moves need to be jerked into place or even executed with speed. Practice going smoothly. And proceed slowly as you approach the end of the move.

- **Communicate about and be conscientious of any injuries you or your partner may have**. Many times, people can continue practicing with a minor injury, as long as both partners are aware of it and compensate for it.

- **Give appropriate resistance when drilling.** When you are first learning a move, it's helpful to work through it slowly, with little resistance, to ensure you hit all of the fine details that make the technique work as intended. As both you and your partner gain familiarity, you can increase the speed of your moves and also work a bit of resistance in your drilling for a realistic sense of how the move works in live action. This should be done at a pace that is comfortable for both you and your training partner.

- **Let the instructor be the instructor.** Partners are not there to teach each other but to learn together. If your partner misses a piece of the instructions, you can point it out. But it is not your job to teach the move. Give feedback when a move feels right on and when it seems to miss the mark. Feedback is different than teaching. Leave teaching to the instructor.

- **Maximize your time on the mat.** Class time is short. Be sure to use it as completely as possible. When you are practicing a move, keep practicing it for the time given by the instructor. If you are wasting practice time, you are also wasting your partner's practice time.

Remember that learning in jiu jitsu only happens with a partner. A good partner makes all the difference in how effectively and safely someone can learn and master jiu jitsu. Be a good partner. And expect your training partners to be good partners. If they are not, give them some feedback on what you would prefer.

HOW TO MAKE
PROGRESS IN JIU JITSU

At some point, every practitioner feels like they are making no progress, and they might even feel stuck. That can be discouraging. Recognize that in those times, something is still happening, and you are improving at a level you might not be noticing. There are also some specific ways you can ensure that you are making the best progress possible, and this section helps with that.

If you want to make progress in jiu jitsu, there is one undeniable necessity: attending class. No matter how many videos, articles, podcasts, or books you consume, there is no substitute for showing up on the mat, getting instruction, and practicing.

But there are factors and choices that can help you make better progress in your jiu jitsu journey. Here are some ways you can make the best progress possible:

- **Find a rhythm for classes and try to stick with it.** You will make better progress the more you attend class. But everyone has a life and obligations outside of the gym, so you need to make sure to find a balance. That said, muscle memory is better facilitated by frequency. The more often you go to class, the more you will learn and retain. If you learn something this week but don't try it again for several weeks, it is far less likely to "stick" than something you learn and repeat within a few days. Consistent attendance is paramount to effective learning.

- **Don't focus on winning or losing, or even being "the best."** Do *your* best. Work to maximize your learning, but don't make it a class competition. Your biggest competitor is not a class member. It is you. Your class members are fellow learners and a resource for getting better, as you are for them.

- **Take notes in class.** Use this journal to maximize your learning. The more you interact with a lesson, the more it will "stick." Showing up for class is the first step. Paying attention is the next step. Taking notes helps you pay attention and retain the information.

- **Review your notes and visualize the moves** from the class not long after that class. Either shortly after class or the next day, read through your notes and picture the moves in your mind, as if you are doing them. Visualizing the moves helps with memory and muscle retention.

- **Always go with "I'll Try."** This doesn't mean you are always confident about a move or taking on a different partner, but it does mean that you will give everything your best shot, that you will "try it out." There will be times when, in a class, you think that you "can't do it." Maybe it is a move, or maybe it is just about making progress. Make a shift to: "I will give it my best and figure it out." When a mindset is "I can't," it blocks the mind from taking in and processing the information. "I will try" opens up possibilities.

- **Use the tap.** It isn't about losing but about learning. The beauty of jiu jitsu is that you can try something without worrying about it working. If it doesn't work, you simply tap and start again. No harm in trying. Don't work to shut down a partner at every turn, as you will never progress to see what you can do at the next turn. If you can't escape, tap. And stretch to try new techniques you are learning. There is no harm in failing a move. You can try something else if it doesn't work. But you are one step closer to it working if you try it.

- **Look for principles, not just moves.** Sure, there are lots of moves with fancy names. But behind the move is a principle. There is something that makes the move work and elements that must be there for it to work.

When you are focused on only the move and it is blocked, you are stuck. But as you learn principles, you can make shifts and even improvise, getting to the same result through a different path. In the beginning, you have to master techniques on your way to principles. Start looking for the principles. Note them in your journal for techniques. They will become clearer as you make progress.

- **Don't go "all out" every time.** Learning is based in "practice/reflection." You try something and reflect on it. When something works, you can think about why it worked. And when something fails, you can think about why it failed. When students go "all out" every time they practice, they don't spend the time with the actual technique, and they don't spend the time on the reflection. Find a comfortable pace.

- **Trust the technique.** As noted earlier, jiu jitsu is based on principles that make the move work. If you are struggling with a move, "muscling through it," it is likely that an element is missing. An angle may be wrong, or a move may be off. You know the move is working when it is efficient—not easy, but efficient. A move should work on an opponent, regardless of their size. If it is not working, before you continue forcing it, try to figure out what is missing.

- **Work with different partners.** Different training partners will expose you to weaknesses in technique as you learn. If you only train with one person, you only learn from that one body type, one style, and one mental approach. Branch out and try different partners for classes and your technique will improve.

- **Don't focus on rank, belts, or stripes.** The belts are not the goal. They simply mark your progress. Focus on making progress and the rank will follow. If you chase a rank, your ego steps in. Your focus ends up being an attempt to "check boxes," not learn technique.

- Most importantly, **leave your ego at the door.** That will keep you safe and help you progress. When ego gets involved, you won't tap when you should. You will be overly critical of yourself and your techniques, you will constantly compare yourself to other students, and you will avoid anything that threatens your ego. That includes not working with lower belts for fear of being tapped, or higher belts for fear of getting tapped. It also includes trying new techniques for fear they will fail. Your ego keeps you from enjoying the process of learning jiu jitsu. Learning requires a lack of ego. So, check your ego at the door and enjoy the process. Progress will come.

HOW TO ROLL FOR YEARS

How long do you want to be involved in jiu jitsu? Are you here for just a little while, wanting to get some extra skills for self-defense? Are you wanting to just try something new? Or do you intend on a longer journey in jiu jitsu? Maybe even to black belt?

The art of jiu jitsu is full of challenge, achievement, skills, comradery, and lessons for life. But to learn them, you will want to be involved for a while, regardless of whether black belt is your goal.

If you want to be in jiu jitsu for the long haul, there are some things you want to do so you can stay involved. And even if you don't intend on doing jiu jitsu for life, you may find your jiu jitsu journey safer and less painful by following these reminders.

Follow these suggestions, and you will be able to keep rolling throughout a long jiu jitsu journey:

- **Focus on "How long can I do this?" rather than "How fast can I get good?"** It is perfectly natural to want to learn a new skill as fast as possible. There is nothing wrong with that wish. If you attend class, pay attention, and practice, you will improve. That is just the outcome of focus and practice. But when your focus is on the speed of getting good,

15

you are likely to go all-out, all the time, which can lead to burnout and injury. So, instead, focus on "how long can I do this?" Remember that Helio Gracie lived to ninety-five and was rolling into his nineties. Lots of people continue into late life. And when that is your focus, you may pace yourself better than when you only attempt to get better faster. Stay rolling longer.

- **Use the tap early and often.** Some people leave jiu jitsu with (or due to) injuries and damage. Often, this is a result of not tapping soon enough. Especially in your early days, tap earlier. While there is a risk of physical injury in any physical activity, among martial arts, jiu jitsu has a lower injury rate due to the tap. When an opponent has you in a lock or a choke, tap and start again. If you can't escape, it is time to tap. (Note: You will want to distinguish between discomfort and the need to tap. For example, if someone is simply controlling their position—say a mount or side mount—it can be uncomfortable but not risky. Learning jiu jitsu is learning to adjust to discomfort. But if your opponent has you in an arm bar or a choke, it is no longer about discomfort. There is now the risk of injury. Time to tap if you don't have an escape.) Play it safer and you will roll longer.

- **Take care of your body between classes.** How you nourish your body, rest your body, and move your body will affect your performance on the mat. If you consume junk food, you are giving junk fuel to your body. If you aren't resting, getting the sleep your body needs, you will be taking more energy than you are giving your body. And while jiu jitsu is great exercise, your body may be well-served by also doing other forms of exercise to balance the strains on your body. Respect your body and you will be better prepared when you are on the mat.

- **Leave your ego at the door.** Jiu jitsu (at least in class) is not about winning, who you tapped, or even who tapped you. The fact is, you will get tapped. Accept that and be willing to tap. Leave your ego at the door and you will roll safer. You will be less likely to refuse to tap. You will also be more likely to recognize when a move is not working, and you will naturally move on to other options and possibilities. When the ego runs your roll, you will force moves (leading to potential injury for your partner and strain/injury for yourself), and you will refuse to tap, unwilling to accept "defeat." Your tap is your safety switch and your learning tool. Use it to learn. Focus less on the win.

- **Practice good hygiene.** A skin infection can derail your class attendance unnecessarily. Jiu jitsu is a sport of close bodily contact and contact with mats that carry risks to your health. But by practicing simple hygiene, you can keep yourself safe (see the section on healthy rolling for specific tips). The healthier you are, the longer you can roll.

- **Practice self-care with partners.** First, remember that you do not have to roll or practice with anyone if you do not want to. You can pass on a roll if you want to, for any reason. If you think that someone is more aggressive than you want, you can pass. If you are concerned about their hygiene, you can pass. If you feel unsafe with them, you can pass. This is not, though, an excuse to pass on people who might be a challenge. It is up to you to make sure you are challenging yourself with different opponents but within a space that feels safe. Challenging is great. Unsafe is not.

- **Give feedback to your partner, both for learning and safety.** Especially in early training, many people are still working to smooth out techniques and determine how far a technique needs to go in order to be effective. Let your partner know before they go too far, as well as when you feel they aren't going far enough or in the right direction. Communication keeps you safe and improves your learning.

- **Focus on your breathing.** In the midst of any strenuous activity, we can easily forget to breathe. This is particularly true when the activity is a martial art. We tend to have some level of fight response when we are practicing any martial art. And part of that response is a tendency to hold your breath. So, always remember to breathe. An easy way to make sure you are breathing is to focus on exhaling. While we tend to hold our breath in, you won't hold your breath out. If you breathe out, you will breathe in.

- **Focus on smooth technique.** Find a pace. Many students focus on speed, not efficiency. Speed hides mistakes and errors that will show up later. If you have a move down, you can do it slowly. And when you are first learning a technique, you will learn it better slowly. You can add some speed once you have the fundamentals. But don't start with speed. Start at a slower pace and work on smooth efficiency. Your learning will improve and your joints (as well as your partner's) will thank you.

- **If you are "all out, all the time," you will burn out and wear out quickly.** There are certainly times when a burst of energy is necessary to cause a shift or catch a move. But if you are going all out all the time, you will simply wear out. Remember that in a real fight, the fighter who is most efficient and able to conserve energy will likely last longer than the person who is in "all-out assault mode." Your task is to outlast the opponent, both in energy and defense. Practice that in practice. You will be better prepared. You will last longer in a particular match and in your overall jiu jitsu journey.

- **Enjoy the journey!** If it isn't fun, look at why. Do you need to practice differently? Do you need to take a little time off? Few people have the opportunity to practice jiu jitsu. Treat it as an honor and enjoy it. Adjust your approach so that you can enjoy it for as long as you can.

HOW TO BEST USE THIS JOURNAL

Now it is time to start using this journal! Welcome to this important part of your jiu jitsu journey. Using this journal will help you progress and learn effectively and efficiently. The journal gives you a way to track your progress, reflect on your learning, and retain your learning along the way.

Take the journal to class with you as often as possible. The more you take it and use it, the more effective it will become—and the more effective you will become as a practitioner.

Learning any new skill can be frustrating as you try to remember the details and different elements. This can definitely be true for jiu jitsu. The purpose of the journal is to allow you to reinforce the details and elements of practice as you write them down, further reinforce them when you reflect on them, and remind you of them when you go back to review at a later time.

A physical skill such as jiu jitsu requires both muscle memory and neural memory. Your body has to go through the moves enough times to understand its role. And your brain has to make the necessary connections for you to retain the details of the move, including applicability and execution. That is where the journal comes in.

How to Use the Journal

Before Class

If you know the technique planned for a particular class, go back and review any entries for that particular move. The longer you maintain your journal, the stronger a resource it becomes. You can mentally rehearse and remind yourself of the technique and details. You can also review the old entries and jot down any questions you might have about the technique on the new lesson page.

On the second page, consider what goals you have for the class and any practice you may be putting in. Your goals may or may not change for each session. It is wise to consider what your goals are, even if the goal is just to enjoy the class. The clearer you are about your goals, the more likely you are to make progress and enjoy the process.

In Class

Be sure to have your journal and a pen or pencil with you in class. You can set it aside when you practice the move. But during instruction, it is wise to have it open, completing the page for the technique as you go.

Start by dating the new page in the journal. This will help you track progress and find a particular lesson later. It will also provide an interesting record of how your understanding of a particular technique and your own application change over time. The same technique will be taught, learned, and understood in different ways each time you are exposed to it.

When a technique is introduced, write down the name of the technique on the indicated line. If you miss the name, simply ask your instructor after class so you can keep a record of it. Also add the name of the instructor teaching it. Over time, you will discover that different instructors give you different viewpoints on the same technique. This will broaden and deepen your understanding of each technique, as well as help you see the teaching styles of different instructors.

In the *Description* area of a page, describe the move and the mechanics of the move. Note the starting positions, the necessary setup, movements, actions, and adjustments that are made during the move execution. If you wish, use drawings to remind you of details that may be missed in your writing. Remember: This is your journal, for your learning. Use it in ways to help you best recall and understand later. As you improve, your journal use will improve too. But getting started with both jiu jitsu and the journal is just a matter of starting. Improving is just about continuing.

In the *Critical Details* section, be sure to highlight anything that is a make-or-break detail that might be overlooked. If you must be positioned in a certain way, or if a setup is necessary, describe it so that you can recall and clarify in your practice.

And in the *Indicator* section, be sure to note the reason for the move. Why would you use this particular technique? What is happening in the roll or the fight that would necessitate the move? In other words, what is an opponent doing that suggests and allows this move? This will help you anchor the move to the reason for the move.

During or at the end of class, fill in the correct tab at the top of the page (for the technique's basic position) and on the edge of the page (for whether the technique is attacking or defensive in nature). Fill in the box all the way to the top and edge of the page. Later, as you fill the journal, you will easily be able to locate all moves from a certain position or all moves for attacking and defending simply by looking for the pages marked at the same point. When you look at the journal from the top or side, you will see all the marked tabs and can pull from your growing arsenal of moves.

On the second page, jot down anything that occurs to you, if time and circumstances allow for it. If not, you can complete it after class is over (but don't wait too long, as our memories of details tend to fade quickly if we don't record soon after).

The *Points to Sharpen* section is where you will make some great progress. What points do you want to particularly pay attention to? Maybe you noticed a tendency to miss a certain element of the move, something that would sharpen the move and make it more effective. Write what you notice down to remember and return to in your practice.

And the *Things to Remember* section is a great place to reflect. What occurred to you when you were in class and practicing? What did you notice about yourself in the class or while using the move? What are those little pieces that are so important for progress but that tend to disappear not long after thinking about them?

After Class

If all you do is use the journal to record the details of a technique during classes, throw it in your bag and only pull it out the next time, it will still serve to improve your retention and help your progress in jiu jitsu.

But you can progress further by going back to your journal page after class. If you can, take a look at it when you get home and cleaned up. If you can't, try to return to it before returning to the next class. Try to build a habit of spending at least five or ten minutes reflecting on class. Using the journal as a guide is a great way to do that.

Read through the description and visualize the move in your mind. Focus on the critical details of the move. And focus on the indicator you are seeing that would cause you to use the move. As you visualize the move, your neuronal links are strengthened and reinforced, helping you to further internalize and memorize the move.

If you have not already, complete the second page for each class. If you practiced in class or after class, record your thoughts. What did you learn? Both about the move and about yourself. What are elements you want to sharpen when you practice again? And what do you want to remember about a technique, a particular session, or about your own progress?

Finally, when you repeat a technique in class, go back to prior notes on that technique and see what you have added or what you understand differently. Jiu jitsu is learned in layers. As you progress, you will begin to see details and layers that were previously missed. This will help deepen your understanding of the simplicity and complexity of each move and of jiu jitsu as art and sport.

Remember that the journal is your own tool. Use it in ways that facilitate your own progress and learning. A tool is only useful when you use it. Be sure and make the journal a habit. Keep on using the journal.

And keep on rolling!

Mount

Side Mount

Guard

Half Guard

Back

Standing

Date: ___/___/____

Technique: _____

Instructor: _____

Attack

Defend

Indicators/Start Point:

_____

Description of Technique:

_____

Critical Details:

Gi

No Gi

Both

# of Practices _____

PRACTICE NOTES

Goals for This Session

1. _____
   _____

2. _____
   _____

3. _____
   _____

Discoveries or Learnings for This Session

1. _____
   _____

2. _____
   _____

3. _____
   _____

_____

Points to Sharpen:

_____

Things to Remember:

The line between disorder and order lies in logistics.
— Sun Tzu

Mount

Side Mount

Guard

Half Guard

Back

Standing

Date: ___/___/____

Technique: _____

Instructor: _____

Attack

Defend

Indicators/Start Point:

_____

Description of Technique:

_____

Critical Details:

Gi

No Gi

Both

# of Practices _____

PRACTICE NOTES

Goals for This Session

1. _____
   _____

2. _____
   _____

3. _____
   _____

Discoveries or Learnings for This Session

1. _____
   _____

2. _____
   _____

3. _____
   _____

_____

Points to Sharpen:

_____

Things to Remember:

You have to build calluses on your brain just like how you build
calluses on your hands. Callus your mind through pain and suffering.
— David Goggins

Mount

Side Mount

Guard

Half Guard

Back

Standing

Date: ___/___/____

Technique: _____

Instructor: _____

Attack

Defend

Indicators/Start Point:

_____

Description of Technique:

_____

Critical Details:

Gi

No Gi

Both

# of Practices _____

PRACTICE NOTES

Goals for This Session

1. _____
   _____
2. _____
   _____
3. _____
   _____

Discoveries or Learnings for This Session

1. _____
   _____
2. _____
   _____
3. _____
   _____

_____

Points to Sharpen:

_____

Things to Remember:

Understand that the essence of martial arts is not
the art itself, but what's hidden deep within yourself.
— Gogen Yamaguchi

Mount

Side Mount

Guard

Half Guard

Back

Standing

Date: ___/___/____

Technique: _____

Instructor: _____

Attack

Defend

Indicators/Start Point:

_____

Description of Technique:

_____

Critical Details:

Gi

No Gi

Both

# of Practices _____

PRACTICE NOTES

Goals for This Session

1. _____
   _____

2. _____
   _____

3. _____
   _____

Discoveries or Learnings for This Session

1. _____
   _____

2. _____
   _____

3. _____
   _____

_____

Points to Sharpen:

_____

Things to Remember:

Our fears don't stop death, they stop life.
— Rickson Gracie

Mount

Side Mount

Guard

Half Guard

Back

Standing

Date: ___/___/____

Technique: _____

Instructor: _____

Attack

Defend

Indicators/Start Point:

_____

Description of Technique:

_____

Critical Details:

Gi

No Gi

Both

# of Practices _____

PRACTICE NOTES

Goals for This Session

1. _____
   _____

2. _____
   _____

3. _____
   _____

Discoveries or Learnings for This Session

1. _____
   _____

2. _____
   _____

3. _____
   _____

_____

Points to Sharpen:

_____

Things to Remember:

Force has no place where there is need of skill.
— Herodotus

Mount

Side Mount

Guard

Half Guard

Back

Standing

Date: ___/___/____

Technique: _____

Instructor: _____

Attack

Defend

Indicators/Start Point:

_____

Description of Technique:

_____

Critical Details:

Gi

No Gi

Both

# of Practices _____

PRACTICE NOTES

Goals for This Session

1. _____
   _____

2. _____
   _____

3. _____
   _____

Discoveries or Learnings for This Session

1. _____
   _____

2. _____
   _____

3. _____
   _____

_____

Points to Sharpen:

_____

Things to Remember:

I never lose. I either win or I learn.
— Nelson Mandela

Mount

Side Mount

Guard

Half Guard

Back

Standing

Date: ___/___/____

Technique: _____

Instructor: _____

Attack

Defend

Indicators/Start Point:

_____

Description of Technique:

_____

Critical Details:

Gi

No Gi

Both

# of Practices _____

PRACTICE NOTES

Goals for This Session

1. _____
   _____
2. _____
   _____
3. _____
   _____

Discoveries or Learnings for This Session

1. _____
   _____
2. _____
   _____
3. _____
   _____

Points to Sharpen:

Things to Remember:

Don't fight your opponent, fight his moves.
— Carlos Gracie Jr.

Mount

Side Mount

Guard

Half Guard

Back

Standing

Date: ___/___/____

Technique: _____

Instructor: _____

Attack

Defend

Indicators/Start Point:

_____

Description of Technique:

_____

Critical Details:

Gi

No Gi

Both

# of Practices _____

PRACTICE NOTES

Goals for This Session

1. _____
   _____
2. _____
   _____
3. _____
   _____

Discoveries or Learnings for This Session

1. _____
   _____
2. _____
   _____
3. _____
   _____

Points to Sharpen:

Things to Remember:

In the fight, only one person can be comfortable. Your job
is to transfer the comfortable from your opponent to you.
— Rickson Gracie

Mount

Side Mount

Guard

Half Guard

Back

Standing

Date: ___/___/____

Technique: _____

Instructor: _____

Attack

Defend

Indicators/Start Point:

_____

Description of Technique:

_____

Critical Details:

Gi

No Gi

Both

# of Practices _____

PRACTICE NOTES

Goals for This Session

1. _____
   _____
2. _____
   _____
3. _____
   _____

Discoveries or Learnings for This Session

1. _____
   _____
2. _____
   _____
3. _____
   _____

Points to Sharpen:

Things to Remember:

My Opponent is my Teacher, my Ego is my Enemy
— Unknown

Mount Side Mount Guard Half Guard Back Standing

Date: ___/___/____

Technique: _____

Instructor: _____

Attack

Defend

Indicators/Start Point:

_____

Description of Technique:

_____

Critical Details:

Gi

No Gi

Both

# of Practices _____

PRACTICE NOTES

Goals for This Session

1. _____
   _____

2. _____
   _____

3. _____
   _____

Discoveries or Learnings for This Session

1. _____
   _____

2. _____
   _____

3. _____
   _____

_____

Points to Sharpen:

_____

Things to Remember:

Martial arts are a vehicle for developing your human potential.
— Joe Rogan

Mount Side Mount Guard Half Guard Back Standing

Date: ___/___/____

Technique: _____

Instructor: _____

Attack ⟨

Defend ⟨

Indicators/Start Point:

_____

Description of Technique:

_____

Critical Details:

Gi ⟨

No Gi ⟨

Both ⟨

# of Practices _____

PRACTICE NOTES

Goals for This Session

1. _____

_____

2. _____

_____

3. _____

_____

Discoveries or Learnings for This Session

1. _____

_____

2. _____

_____

3. _____

_____

Points to Sharpen:

Things to Remember:

We are what we repeatedly do. Excellence then, is not an act, but a habit.
— Aristotle

Mount

Side Mount

Guard

Half Guard

Back

Standing

Date: ___/___/____

Technique: _____

Instructor: _____

Attack

Defend

Indicators/Start Point:

_____

Description of Technique:

_____

Critical Details:

Gi

No Gi

Both

# of Practices _____

PRACTICE NOTES

Goals for This Session

1. _____
   _____
2. _____
   _____
3. _____
   _____

Discoveries or Learnings for This Session

1. _____
   _____
2. _____
   _____
3. _____
   _____

Points to Sharpen:

Things to Remember:

Jiu jitsu is not the art of hitting, it's the art of not getting hit
— Royce Gracie

Mount Side Mount Guard Half Guard Back Standing

Date: ___/___/____

Technique: _____

Instructor: _____

Attack

Defend

Indicators/Start Point:

_____

Description of Technique:

_____

Critical Details:

Gi

No Gi

Both

# of Practices _____

PRACTICE NOTES

Goals for This Session

1. _____
   _____
2. _____
   _____
3. _____
   _____

Discoveries or Learnings for This Session

1. _____
   _____
2. _____
   _____
3. _____
   _____

Points to Sharpen:

Things to Remember:

In the midst of chaos, there is also opportunity.
— Sun Tzu

Mount
Side Mount
Guard
Half Guard
Back
Standing

Date: ___/___/____

Technique: _____

Instructor: _____

Attack

Defend

Indicators/Start Point:

_____

Description of Technique:

_____

Critical Details:

Gi

No Gi

Both

# of Practices _____

PRACTICE NOTES

Goals for This Session

1. _____

2. _____

3. _____

Discoveries or Learnings for This Session

1. _____

2. _____

3. _____

Points to Sharpen:

Things to Remember:

You just can't beat the person who never gives up.
— Babe Ruth

Mount

Side Mount

Guard

Half Guard

Back

Standing

Date: ___/___/____

Technique: _____

Instructor: _____

Attack

Defend

Indicators/Start Point:

_____

Description of Technique:

_____

Critical Details:

Gi

No Gi

Both

# of Practices _____

PRACTICE NOTES

Goals for This Session

1. _____
   _____
2. _____
   _____
3. _____
   _____

Discoveries or Learnings for This Session

1. _____
   _____
2. _____
   _____
3. _____
   _____

Points to Sharpen:

Things to Remember:

Strategy without tactics is the slowest route to victory.
Tactics without strategy is the noise before defeat.
— Sun Tzu

Mount

Side Mount

Guard

Half Guard

Back

Standing

Date: ___/___/____

Technique: _____

Instructor: _____

Attack

Defend

Indicators/Start Point:

_____

Description of Technique:

_____

Critical Details:

Gi

No Gi

Both

# of Practices _____

PRACTICE NOTES

Goals for This Session

1. _____
   _____

2. _____
   _____

3. _____
   _____

Discoveries or Learnings for This Session

1. _____
   _____

2. _____
   _____

3. _____
   _____

_____

Points to Sharpen:

_____

Things to Remember:

All martial arts is simply an honest expression
of one's body with a lot of deception in between.
— Bruce Lee

Mount

Side Mount

Guard

Half Guard

Back

Standing

Date: ___/___/____

Technique: _____

Instructor: _____

Attack

Defend

Indicators/Start Point:

_____

Description of Technique:

_____

Critical Details:

Gi

No Gi

Both

# of Practices _____

PRACTICE NOTES

Goals for This Session

1. _____
   _____

2. _____
   _____

3. _____
   _____

Discoveries or Learnings for This Session

1. _____
   _____

2. _____
   _____

3. _____
   _____

_____

Points to Sharpen:

_____

Things to Remember:

*Understand that the essence of martial arts is not
the art itself, but what's hidden deep within yourself.*
— Gogen Yamaguchi

Mount

Side Mount

Guard

Half Guard

Back

Standing

Date: ___/___/____

Technique: _____

Instructor: _____

Attack

Defend

Indicators/Start Point:

_____

Description of Technique:

_____

Critical Details:

Gi

No Gi

Both

# of Practices _____

PRACTICE NOTES

Goals for This Session

1. _____
   _____
2. _____
   _____
3. _____
   _____

Discoveries or Learnings for This Session

1. _____
   _____
2. _____
   _____
3. _____
   _____

Points to Sharpen:

Things to Remember:

Don't worry about the elements around you and
what's going on. You gotta get out there and get it.
— David Goggins

Mount

Side Mount

Guard

Half Guard

Back

Standing

Date: ___/___/____

Technique: _____

Instructor: _____

Attack

Defend

Indicators/Start Point:

_____

Description of Technique:

_____

Critical Details:

Gi

No Gi

Both

# of Practices _____

PRACTICE NOTES

Goals for This Session

1. _____
   _____

2. _____
   _____

3. _____
   _____

Discoveries or Learnings for This Session

1. _____
   _____

2. _____
   _____

3. _____
   _____

Points to Sharpen:

Things to Remember:

Remember you are expressing the technique, not doing the technique.
— Bruce Lee

Mount

Side Mount

Guard

Half Guard

Back

Standing

Date: ___/___/____

Technique: _____

Instructor: _____

Attack (

Defend (

Indicators/Start Point:

_____

Description of Technique:

_____

Critical Details:

Gi (

No Gi (

Both (

# of Practices _____

PRACTICE NOTES

Goals for This Session

1. _____
_____
2. _____
_____
3. _____
_____

Discoveries or Learnings for This Session

1. _____
_____
2. _____
_____
3. _____
_____

_____

Points to Sharpen:

_____

Things to Remember:

Opportunities multiply as they are seized.
— Sun Tzu

Mount

Side Mount

Guard

Half Guard

Back

Standing

Date: ___/___/____

Technique: _____

Instructor: _____

Attack

Defend

Indicators/Start Point:

_____

Description of Technique:

_____

Critical Details:

Gi

No Gi

Both

# of Practices _____

PRACTICE NOTES

Goals for This Session

1. _____
   _____
2. _____
   _____
3. _____
   _____

Discoveries or Learnings for This Session

1. _____
   _____
2. _____
   _____
3. _____
   _____

Points to Sharpen:

Things to Remember:

Never interrupt your enemy when he is making a mistake.
— Napoleon Bonaparte

Mount　Side Mount　Guard　Half Guard　Back　Standing

Date: ___/___/____

Technique: _____

Instructor: _____

Attack

Defend

Indicators/Start Point:

_____

Description of Technique:

_____

Critical Details:

Gi

No Gi

Both

# of Practices _____

PRACTICE NOTES

Goals for This Session

1. _____
   _____

2. _____
   _____

3. _____
   _____

Discoveries or Learnings for This Session

1. _____
   _____

2. _____
   _____

3. _____
   _____

_____

Points to Sharpen:

_____

Things to Remember:

Those skilled in warfare move the enemy, and are not moved by the enemy.
— Sun Tzu

Mount Side Mount Guard Half Guard Back Standing

Date: ___/___/____

Technique: _____

Instructor: _____

Attack

Defend

Indicators/Start Point:

_____

Description of Technique:

_____

Critical Details:

Gi

No Gi

Both

# of Practices _____

PRACTICE NOTES

Goals for This Session

1. _____
   _____
2. _____
   _____
3. _____
   _____

Discoveries or Learnings for This Session

1. _____
   _____
2. _____
   _____
3. _____
   _____

Points to Sharpen:

Things to Remember:

*Martial arts is not about picking your fights and picking
how things go; it's about adapting to the how things are.*
— Gunnar Nelson

Mount Side Mount Guard Half Guard Back Standing

Date: ___/___/____

Technique: _____

Instructor: _____

Attack ⟨

Defend ⟨

Indicators/Start Point:

_____

Description of Technique:

_____

Critical Details:

Gi ⟨

No Gi ⟨

Both ⟨

# of Practices _____

PRACTICE NOTES

Goals for This Session

1. _____
   _____

2. _____
   _____

3. _____
   _____

Discoveries or Learnings for This Session

1. _____
   _____

2. _____
   _____

3. _____
   _____

_____

Points to Sharpen:

_____

Things to Remember:

You win battles by knowing the enemy's timing,
and using a timing that the enemy does not expect.
— Miyamoto Musashi

Mount

Side Mount

Guard

Half Guard

Back

Standing

Date: ___/___/____

Technique: _____

Instructor: _____

Attack ⟨

Defend ⟨

Indicators/Start Point:

_____

Description of Technique:

_____

Critical Details:

Gi ⟨

No Gi ⟨

Both ⟨

# of Practices _____

PRACTICE NOTES

Goals for This Session

1. _____
   _____

2. _____
   _____

3. _____
   _____

Discoveries or Learnings for This Session

1. _____
   _____

2. _____
   _____

3. _____
   _____

Points to Sharpen:

Things to Remember:

In jiu jitsu, we often fall into the trap of simply trying a technique harder,
rather than recognizing that it is a poorly chosen tool for the task at hand.
— Chris Matakas

Mount

Side Mount

Guard

Half Guard

Back

Standing

Date: ___/___/____

Technique: _____

Instructor: _____

Attack

Defend

Indicators/Start Point:

_____

Description of Technique:

_____

Critical Details:

Gi

No Gi

Both

# of Practices _____

PRACTICE NOTES

Goals for This Session

1. _____

    _____

2. _____

    _____

3. _____

    _____

Discoveries or Learnings for This Session

1. _____

    _____

2. _____

    _____

3. _____

    _____

_____

Points to Sharpen:

_____

Things to Remember:

Victory comes from finding opportunities in problems.
— Sun Tzu

Mount

Side Mount

Guard

Half Guard

Back

Standing

Date: ___/___/____

Technique: _____

Instructor: _____

Attack

Defend

Indicators/Start Point:

_____

Description of Technique:

_____

Critical Details:

Gi

No Gi

Both

# of Practices _____

PRACTICE NOTES

Goals for This Session

1. _____
_____

2. _____
_____

3. _____
_____

Discoveries or Learnings for This Session

1. _____
_____

2. _____
_____

3. _____
_____

_____

Points to Sharpen:

_____

Things to Remember:

In martial arts, the biggest enemy is self. Inside
you struggle because you want to prove something.
— Jet Li

Mount

Side Mount

Guard

Half Guard

Back

Standing

Date: ___/___/____

Technique: _____

Instructor: _____

Attack

Defend

Indicators/Start Point:

_____

Description of Technique:

_____

Critical Details:

Gi

No Gi

Both

# of Practices _____

PRACTICE NOTES

Goals for This Session

1. _____
   _____

2. _____
   _____

3. _____
   _____

Discoveries or Learnings for This Session

1. _____
   _____

2. _____
   _____

3. _____
   _____

_____

Points to Sharpen:

_____

Things to Remember:

I see martial arts as moving forms of meditation. When you're
sparring or drilling techniques, you can't think of anything else.
— Joe Rogan

Mount | Side Mount | Guard | Half Guard | Back | Standing

Date: ___/___/____

Technique: _____

Instructor: _____

Attack

Defend

Indicators/Start Point:

_____

Description of Technique:

_____

Critical Details:

Gi

No Gi

Both

# of Practices _____

PRACTICE NOTES

Goals for This Session

1. _____
   _____
2. _____
   _____
3. _____
   _____

Discoveries or Learnings for This Session

1. _____
   _____
2. _____
   _____
3. _____
   _____

_____

Points to Sharpen:

_____

Things to Remember:

Strength is not born from strength. Strength can be born only from weakness.
So be glad of your weaknesses now, they are the beginnings of your strength.
— Claire Weekes

Mount

Side Mount

Guard

Half Guard

Back

Standing

Date: ___/___/____

Technique: _____

Instructor: _____

Attack

Defend

Indicators/Start Point:

_____

Description of Technique:

_____

Critical Details:

Gi

No Gi

Both

# of Practices _____

PRACTICE NOTES

Goals for This Session

1. _____
   _____
2. _____
   _____
3. _____
   _____

Discoveries or Learnings for This Session

1. _____
   _____
2. _____
   _____
3. _____
   _____

_____

Points to Sharpen:

_____

Things to Remember:

The true work of the martial arts is progress, not perfection.
— Gene Dunn

Mount

Side Mount

Guard

Half Guard

Back

Standing

Date: ___/___/____

Technique: _____

Instructor: _____

Attack

Defend

Indicators/Start Point:

_____

Description of Technique:

_____

Critical Details:

Gi

No Gi

Both

# of Practices _____

PRACTICE NOTES

Goals for This Session

1. _____
   _____
2. _____
   _____
3. _____
   _____

Discoveries or Learnings for This Session

1. _____
   _____
2. _____
   _____
3. _____
   _____

_____

Points to Sharpen:

_____

Things to Remember:

I fear not the man who has practiced 10,000 kicks once
but I fear the man who has practiced one kick 10,000 times.
— Bruce Lee

Mount

Side Mount

Guard

Half Guard

Back

Standing

Date: ___/___/____

Technique: _____

Instructor: _____

Attack

Defend

Indicators/Start Point:

_____

Description of Technique:

_____

Critical Details:

Gi

No Gi

Both

# of Practices _____

PRACTICE NOTES

Goals for This Session

1. _____

2. _____

3. _____

Discoveries or Learnings for This Session

1. _____

2. _____

3. _____

Points to Sharpen:

Things to Remember:

The best fighter is never angry.
— Lao Tzu

Mount

Side Mount

Guard

Half Guard

Back

Standing

Date: ___/___/____

Technique: _____

Instructor: _____

Attack

Defend

Indicators/Start Point:

_____

Description of Technique:

_____

Critical Details:

Gi

No Gi

Both

# of Practices _____

PRACTICE NOTES

Goals for This Session

1. _____
   _____

2. _____
   _____

3. _____
   _____

Discoveries or Learnings for This Session

1. _____
   _____

2. _____
   _____

3. _____
   _____

_____

Points to Sharpen:

_____

Things to Remember:

*A black belt is nothing more than a belt, a piece of cloth. Your ultimate
goal should not be to get your black belt. Your ultimate goal should be to
be a black belt. Being a black belt is a state of mind, a way of life.*
— Bohdi Sanders

Mount

Side Mount

Guard

Half Guard

Back

Standing

Date: ___/___/____

Technique: _____

Instructor: _____

Attack

Defend

Indicators/Start Point:

_____

Description of Technique:

_____

Critical Details:

Gi

No Gi

Both

# of Practices _____

PRACTICE NOTES

Goals for This Session

1. _____
   _____

2. _____
   _____

3. _____
   _____

Discoveries or Learnings for This Session

1. _____
   _____

2. _____
   _____

3. _____
   _____

Points to Sharpen:

Things to Remember:

*True mastery, it turns out, is not found in accumulating each
and every tool under the sun. True mastery is learning that there
are really only a handful of tools, and it is the proper application
with correct timing and setting that makes them so useful.*
— Chris Matakas

Mount

Side Mount

Guard

Half Guard

Back

Standing

Date: ___/___/____

Technique: _____

Instructor: _____

Attack

Defend

Indicators/Start Point:

_____

Description of Technique:

_____

Critical Details:

Gi

No Gi

Both

# of Practices _____

PRACTICE NOTES

Goals for This Session

1. _____
   _____

2. _____
   _____

3. _____
   _____

Discoveries or Learnings for This Session

1. _____
   _____

2. _____
   _____

3. _____
   _____

_____

Points to Sharpen:

_____

Things to Remember:

Never forget that, at the most, the teacher can give you fifteen percent
of the art. The rest you have to get for yourself through practise and
hard work. I can show you the path but I can not walk it for you.
— Master Tan Soh Tin

Mount

Side Mount

Guard

Half Guard

Back

Standing

Date: ___/___/____

Technique: _____

Instructor: _____

Attack

Defend

Indicators/Start Point:

_____

Description of Technique:

_____

Critical Details:

Gi

No Gi

Both

# of Practices _____

PRACTICE NOTES

Goals for This Session

1. _____
   _____
2. _____
   _____
3. _____
   _____

Discoveries or Learnings for This Session

1. _____
   _____
2. _____
   _____
3. _____
   _____

_____

Points to Sharpen:

_____

Things to Remember:

The supreme art of war is to subdue the enemy without fighting.
— Sun Tzu

Mount

Side Mount

Guard

Half Guard

Back

Standing

Date: ___/___/____

Technique: _____

Instructor: _____

Attack ⟨

Defend ⟨

Indicators/Start Point:

_____

Description of Technique:

_____

Critical Details:

Gi ⟨

No Gi ⟨

Both ⟨

# of Practices _____

PRACTICE NOTES

Goals for This Session

1. _____
   _____

2. _____
   _____

3. _____
   _____

Discoveries or Learnings for This Session

1. _____
   _____

2. _____
   _____

3. _____
   _____

_____

Points to Sharpen:

_____

Things to Remember:

A warrior may choose pacifism; others are condemned to it.
— Author unknown

Mount

Side Mount

Guard

Half Guard

Back

Standing

Date: ___/___/____

Technique: _____

Instructor: _____

Attack

Defend

Indicators/Start Point:

_____

Description of Technique:

_____

Critical Details:

Gi

No Gi

Both

# of Practices _____

PRACTICE NOTES

Goals for This Session

1. _____
   _____
2. _____
   _____
3. _____
   _____

Discoveries or Learnings for This Session

1. _____
   _____
2. _____
   _____
3. _____
   _____

_____

Points to Sharpen:

_____

Things to Remember:

However beautiful the strategy, you should occasionally look at the results
— Sir Winston Churchill

Mount

Side Mount

Guard

Half Guard

Back

Standing

Date: ___/___/_____

Technique: _____

Instructor: _____

Attack

Defend

Indicators/Start Point:

_____

Description of Technique:

_____

Critical Details:

Gi

No Gi

Both

# of Practices _____

PRACTICE NOTES

Goals for This Session

1. _____
   _____
2. _____
   _____
3. _____
   _____

Discoveries or Learnings for This Session

1. _____
   _____
2. _____
   _____
3. _____
   _____

_____

Points to Sharpen:

_____

Things to Remember:

In the struggle between the stone and water, in time, the water wins
— Japanese Proverb

Mount

Side Mount

Guard

Half Guard

Back

Standing

Date: ___/___/____

Technique: _____

Instructor: _____

Attack

Defend

Indicators/Start Point:

_____

Description of Technique:

_____

Critical Details:

Gi

No Gi

Both

# of Practices _____

PRACTICE NOTES

Goals for This Session

1. _____
   _____

2. _____
   _____

3. _____
   _____

Discoveries or Learnings for This Session

1. _____
   _____

2. _____
   _____

3. _____
   _____

_____

Points to Sharpen:

_____

Things to Remember:

I've found that luck is quite predictable. If you want more luck,
take more chances. Be more active. Show up more often.
— Brian Tracy

Mount

Side Mount

Guard

Half Guard

Back

Standing

Date: ___/___/____

Technique: _____

Instructor: _____

Attack

Defend

Indicators/Start Point:

_____

Description of Technique:

_____

Critical Details:

Gi

No Gi

Both

# of Practices _____

PRACTICE NOTES

Goals for This Session

1. _____
   _____
2. _____
   _____
3. _____
   _____

Discoveries or Learnings for This Session

1. _____
   _____
2. _____
   _____
3. _____
   _____

_____

Points to Sharpen:

_____

Things to Remember:

It is more important to out-think your enemy, than to outfight him
— Sun Tzu

Mount

Side Mount

Guard

Half Guard

Back

Standing

Date: ___/___/____

Technique: _____

Instructor: _____

Attack

Defend

Indicators/Start Point:

_____

Description of Technique:

_____

Critical Details:

Gi

No Gi

Both

# of Practices _____

PRACTICE NOTES

Goals for This Session

1. _____
   _____
2. _____
   _____
3. _____
   _____

Discoveries or Learnings for This Session

1. _____
   _____
2. _____
   _____
3. _____
   _____

Points to Sharpen:

Things to Remember:

There is no comfort in the growth zone and no growth in the comfort zone
— Unknown

Mount

Side Mount

Guard

Half Guard

Back

Standing

Date: ___/___/____

Technique: _____

Instructor: _____

Attack

Defend

Indicators/Start Point:

_____

Description of Technique:

_____

Critical Details:

Gi

No Gi

Both

# of Practices _____

PRACTICE NOTES

Goals for This Session

1. _____
   _____
2. _____
   _____
3. _____
   _____

Discoveries or Learnings for This Session

1. _____
   _____
2. _____
   _____
3. _____
   _____

_____

Points to Sharpen:

_____

Things to Remember:

Learning defense improves the attack. If the lion knows how
the prey can escape, it'll capture it in a much more precise way
— Rillion Gracie

Mount

Side Mount

Guard

Half Guard

Back

Standing

Date: ___/___/____

Technique: _____

Instructor: _____

Attack ⟨

Defend ⟨

Indicators/Start Point:

_____

Description of Technique:

_____

Critical Details:

Gi ⟨

No Gi ⟨

Both ⟨

# of Practices _____

PRACTICE NOTES

Goals for This Session

1. _____
   _____

2. _____
   _____

3. _____
   _____

Discoveries or Learnings for This Session

1. _____
   _____

2. _____
   _____

3. _____
   _____

_____

Points to Sharpen:

_____

Things to Remember:

Fall down 7 times, get up 8 times.
— Japanese maxim

Mount

Side Mount

Guard

Half Guard

Back

Standing

Date: ___/___/____

Technique: _____

Instructor: _____

Attack (

Defend (

Indicators/Start Point:

_____

Description of Technique:

_____

Critical Details:

Gi (

No Gi (

Both (

# of Practices _____

PRACTICE NOTES

Goals for This Session

1. _____
   _____

2. _____
   _____

3. _____
   _____

Discoveries or Learnings for This Session

1. _____
   _____

2. _____
   _____

3. _____
   _____

_____

Points to Sharpen:

_____

Things to Remember:

Appear weak when you are strong, and strong when you are weak.
— Sun Tzu

Mount   Side Mount   Guard   Half Guard   Back   Standing

Date: ___/___/____

Technique: _____

Instructor: _____

Attack

Defend

Indicators/Start Point:

_____

Description of Technique:

_____

Critical Details:

Gi

No Gi

Both

# of Practices _____

PRACTICE NOTES

Goals for This Session

1. _____
   _____
2. _____
   _____
3. _____
   _____

Discoveries or Learnings for This Session

1. _____
   _____
2. _____
   _____
3. _____
   _____

_____

Points to Sharpen:

_____

Things to Remember:

Obey the principles without being bound by them.
— Bruce Lee

Mount | Side Mount | Guard | Half Guard | Back | Standing

Date: ___/___/____

Technique: _____

Instructor: _____

Attack ⟨

Defend ⟨

Indicators/Start Point:

_____

Description of Technique:

_____

Critical Details:

Gi ⟨

No Gi ⟨

Both ⟨

# of Practices _____

PRACTICE NOTES

Goals for This Session

1. _____
   _____

2. _____
   _____

3. _____
   _____

Discoveries or Learnings for This Session

1. _____
   _____

2. _____
   _____

3. _____
   _____

_____

Points to Sharpen:

_____

Things to Remember:

Learning is never cumulative, it is a movement
of knowing which has no beginning and no end.
— Bruce Lee

Mount

Side Mount

Guard

Half Guard

Back

Standing

Date: ___/___/____

Technique: _____

Instructor: _____

Attack

Defend

Indicators/Start Point:

_____

Description of Technique:

_____

Critical Details:

Gi

No Gi

Both

# of Practices _____

PRACTICE NOTES

Goals for This Session

1. _____
   _____
2. _____
   _____
3. _____
   _____

Discoveries or Learnings for This Session

1. _____
   _____
2. _____
   _____
3. _____
   _____

_____

Points to Sharpen:

_____

Things to Remember:

Put one foot in front of the other, focus on the little goal
right in front of you, and almost anything is possible.
— Joe De Sena

Mount

Side Mount

Guard

Half Guard

Back

Standing

Date: ___/___/____

Technique: _____

Instructor: _____

Attack <

Defend <

Indicators/Start Point:

_____

Description of Technique:

_____

Critical Details:

Gi <

No Gi <

Both <

# of Practices _____

PRACTICE NOTES

Goals for This Session

1. _____
   _____

2. _____
   _____

3. _____
   _____

Discoveries or Learnings for This Session

1. _____
   _____

2. _____
   _____

3. _____
   _____

_____

Points to Sharpen:

_____

Things to Remember:

When you get really good at something as difficult
as Jiu Jitsu, it makes everything in your life better.
— Joe Rogan

Mount | Side Mount | Guard | Half Guard | Back | Standing

Date: ___/___/____

Technique: _____

Instructor: _____

Attack

Defend

Indicators/Start Point:

_____

Description of Technique:

_____

Critical Details:

Gi

No Gi

Both

# of Practices _____

PRACTICE NOTES

Goals for This Session

1. _____
   _____
2. _____
   _____
3. _____
   _____

Discoveries or Learnings for This Session

1. _____
   _____
2. _____
   _____
3. _____
   _____

_____

Points to Sharpen:

_____

Things to Remember:

Without continual growth and progress, such words as
improvement, achievement, and success have no meaning.
— Benjamin Franklin

Mount

Side Mount

Guard

Half Guard

Back

Standing

Date: ___/___/____

Technique: _____

Instructor: _____

Attack

Defend

Indicators/Start Point:

_____

Description of Technique:

_____

Critical Details:

Gi

No Gi

Both

# of Practices _____

PRACTICE NOTES

Goals for This Session

1. _____
   _____

2. _____
   _____

3. _____
   _____

Discoveries or Learnings for This Session

1. _____
   _____

2. _____
   _____

3. _____
   _____

_____

Points to Sharpen:

_____

Things to Remember:

Failure will never overtake me if my
determination to succeed is strong enough.
— Og Mandino

Mount

Side Mount

Guard

Half Guard

Back

Standing

Date: ___/___/____

Technique: _____

Instructor: _____

Attack

Defend

Indicators/Start Point:

_____

Description of Technique:

_____

Critical Details:

Gi

No Gi

Both

# of Practices _____

PRACTICE NOTES

Goals for This Session

1. _____
   _____

2. _____
   _____

3. _____
   _____

Discoveries or Learnings for This Session

1. _____
   _____

2. _____
   _____

3. _____
   _____

Points to Sharpen:

Things to Remember:

Concentrate your energy and hoard your strength.
— Sun Tzu

Mount | Side Mount | Guard | Half Guard | Back | Standing

Date: ___/___/____

Technique: _____

Instructor: _____

Attack ⟨

Defend ⟨

Indicators/Start Point:

_____

Description of Technique:

_____

Critical Details:

Gi ⟨

No Gi ⟨

Both ⟨

# of Practices _____

PRACTICE NOTES

Goals for This Session

1. _____
   _____

2. _____
   _____

3. _____
   _____

Discoveries or Learnings for This Session

1. _____
   _____

2. _____
   _____

3. _____
   _____

_____

Points to Sharpen:

_____

Things to Remember:

When you realize you are no longer made of glass,
you lose the desire to demonstrate that fragility in others.
— Chris Matakas

Mount

Side Mount

Guard

Half Guard

Back

Standing

Date: ___/___/____

Technique: _____

Instructor: _____

Attack

Defend

Indicators/Start Point:

_____

Description of Technique:

_____

Critical Details:

Gi

No Gi

Both

# of Practices _____

PRACTICE NOTES

Goals for This Session

1. _____
   _____
2. _____
   _____
3. _____
   _____

Discoveries or Learnings for This Session

1. _____
   _____
2. _____
   _____
3. _____
   _____

_____

Points to Sharpen:

_____

Things to Remember:

What you get by achieving your goals is not as
important as what you become by achieving your goals.
— Henry David Thoreau

Mount

Side Mount

Guard

Half Guard

Back

Standing

Date: ___/___/____

Technique: _____

Instructor: _____

Attack

Defend

Indicators/Start Point:

_____

Description of Technique:

_____

Critical Details:

Gi

No Gi

Both

# of Practices _____

PRACTICE NOTES

Goals for This Session

1. _____
   _____
2. _____
   _____
3. _____
   _____

Discoveries or Learnings for This Session

1. _____
   _____
2. _____
   _____
3. _____
   _____

_____

Points to Sharpen:

_____

Things to Remember:

Never give up on a dream just because of the time it
will take to accomplish it. The time will pass anyway.
— Earl Nightingale

Mount

Side Mount

Guard

Half Guard

Back

Standing

Date: ___/___/____

Technique: _____

Instructor: _____

Attack (

Defend (

Indicators/Start Point:

_____

Description of Technique:

_____

Critical Details:

Gi (

No Gi (

Both (

# of Practices _____

PRACTICE NOTES

Goals for This Session

1. _____
   _____
2. _____
   _____
3. _____
   _____

Discoveries or Learnings for This Session

1. _____
   _____
2. _____
   _____
3. _____
   _____

_____

Points to Sharpen:

_____

Things to Remember:

Avoiding failure is to avoid progress.
— Author Unknown

Mount

Side Mount

Guard

Half Guard

Back

Standing

Date: ___/___/____

Technique: _____

Instructor: _____

Attack

Defend

Indicators/Start Point:

_____

Description of Technique:

_____

Critical Details:

Gi

No Gi

Both

# of Practices _____

PRACTICE NOTES

Goals for This Session

1. _____
_____
2. _____
_____
3. _____
_____

Discoveries or Learnings for This Session

1. _____
_____
2. _____
_____
3. _____
_____

_____

Points to Sharpen:

_____

Things to Remember:

Others can stop you temporarily—you are
the only one who can do it permanently.
— Zig Ziglar

Mount | Side Mount | Guard | Half Guard | Back | Standing

Date: ___/___/____

Technique: _____

Instructor: _____

Attack

Defend

Indicators/Start Point:

_____

Description of Technique:

_____

Critical Details:

Gi

No Gi

Both

# of Practices _____

PRACTICE NOTES

Goals for This Session

1. _____
   _____
2. _____
   _____
3. _____
   _____

Discoveries or Learnings for This Session

1. _____
   _____
2. _____
   _____
3. _____
   _____

_____

Points to Sharpen:

_____

Things to Remember:

He who is not courageous enough to take risks will accomplish nothing in life.
— Muhammad Ali

Mount Side Mount Guard Half Guard Back Standing

Date: ___/___/____

Technique: _____

Instructor: _____

Attack ⟨

Defend ⟨

Indicators/Start Point:

_____

Description of Technique:

_____

Critical Details:

Gi ⟨

No Gi ⟨

Both ⟨

# of Practices _____

PRACTICE NOTES

Goals for This Session

1. _____
   _____
2. _____
   _____
3. _____
   _____

Discoveries or Learnings for This Session

1. _____
   _____
2. _____
   _____
3. _____
   _____

_____

Points to Sharpen:

_____

Things to Remember:

Inaction breeds doubt and fear. Action breeds confidence and courage. If you want to conquer fear, do not sit home and think about it. Go out and get busy.
— Dale Carnegie

Mount
Side Mount
Guard
Half Guard
Back
Standing

Date: ___/___/____

Technique: _____

Instructor: _____

Attack ⟨

Defend ⟨

Indicators/Start Point:

_____

Description of Technique:

_____

Critical Details:

Gi ⟨

No Gi ⟨

Both ⟨

# of Practices _____

PRACTICE NOTES

Goals for This Session

1. _____
   _____
2. _____
   _____
3. _____
   _____

Discoveries or Learnings for This Session

1. _____
   _____
2. _____
   _____
3. _____
   _____

_____

Points to Sharpen:

_____

Things to Remember:

Learning is not attained by chance, it must be
sought for with ardor and attended to with diligence:
— Abigail Adams

Mount

Side Mount

Guard

Half Guard

Back

Standing

Date: ___/___/____

Technique: _____

Instructor: _____

Attack

Defend

Indicators/Start Point:

_____

Description of Technique:

_____

Critical Details:

Gi

No Gi

Both

# of Practices _____

PRACTICE NOTES

Goals for This Session

1. _____

   _____

2. _____

   _____

3. _____

   _____

Discoveries or Learnings for This Session

1. _____

   _____

2. _____

   _____

3. _____

   _____

Points to Sharpen:

Things to Remember:

Be curious, not judgemental
— Walt Whitman

Mount Side Mount Guard Half Guard Back Standing

Date: ___/___/____

Technique: _____

Instructor: _____

Attack

Defend

Indicators/Start Point:

_____

Description of Technique:

_____

Critical Details:

Gi

No Gi

Both

# of Practices _____

PRACTICE NOTES

Goals for This Session

1. _____
   _____
2. _____
   _____
3. _____
   _____

Discoveries or Learnings for This Session

1. _____
   _____
2. _____
   _____
3. _____
   _____

_____

Points to Sharpen:

_____

Things to Remember:

Tell me and I forget. Teach me and I remember. Involve me and I learn.
— Benjamin Franklin

Mount Side Mount Guard Half Guard Back Standing

Date: ___/___/____

Technique: _____

Instructor: _____

Attack ⟨

Defend ⟨

Indicators/Start Point:

_____

Description of Technique:

_____

Critical Details:

Gi ⟨

No Gi ⟨

Both ⟨

# of Practices _____

PRACTICE NOTES

Goals for This Session

1. _____
   _____

2. _____
   _____

3. _____
   _____

Discoveries or Learnings for This Session

1. _____
   _____

2. _____
   _____

3. _____
   _____

Points to Sharpen:

Things to Remember:

Empty your mind, be formless, shapeless—like water. Now you
put water in a cup, it becomes the cup; You put water into a
bottle it becomes the bottle; You put it in a teapot it becomes the
teapot. Now water can flow or it can crash. Be water, my friend.
— Bruce Lee

Mount

Side Mount

Guard

Half Guard

Back

Standing

Date: ___/___/____

Technique: _____

Instructor: _____

Attack

Defend

Indicators/Start Point:

_____

Description of Technique:

_____

Critical Details:

Gi

No Gi

Both

# of Practices _____

PRACTICE NOTES

Goals for This Session

1. _____
   _____

2. _____
   _____

3. _____
   _____

Discoveries or Learnings for This Session

1. _____
   _____

2. _____
   _____

3. _____
   _____

_____

Points to Sharpen:

_____

Things to Remember:

Do not judge me by my success, judge me by
how many times I fell down and got back up again.
— Nelson Mandela

Mount

Side Mount

Guard

Half Guard

Back

Standing

Date: ___/___/____

Technique: _____

Instructor: _____

Attack ⟨

Defend ⟨

Indicators/Start Point:

_____

Description of Technique:

_____

Critical Details:

Gi ⟨

No Gi ⟨

Both ⟨

# of Practices _____

PRACTICE NOTES

Goals for This Session

1. _____
   _____
2. _____
   _____
3. _____
   _____

Discoveries or Learnings for This Session

1. _____
   _____
2. _____
   _____
3. _____
   _____

_____

Points to Sharpen:

_____

Things to Remember:

Forgive yourself for your faults and your mistakes and move on.
— Les Brown

Mount Side Mount Guard Half Guard Back Standing

Date: ___/___/____

Technique: _____

Instructor: _____

Attack

Defend

Indicators/Start Point:

_____

Description of Technique:

_____

Critical Details:

Gi

No Gi

Both

# of Practices _____

PRACTICE NOTES

Goals for This Session

1. _____
   _____

2. _____
   _____

3. _____
   _____

Discoveries or Learnings for This Session

1. _____
   _____

2. _____
   _____

3. _____
   _____

_____

Points to Sharpen:

_____

Things to Remember:

The real glory is being knocked to your knees and then
coming back. That's real glory. That's the essence of it.
— Vince Lombardi

Mount

Side Mount

Guard

Half Guard

Back

Standing

Date: ___/___/____

Technique: _____

Instructor: _____

Attack

Defend

Indicators/Start Point:

_____

Description of Technique:

_____

Critical Details:

Gi

No Gi

Both

# of Practices _____

PRACTICE NOTES

Goals for This Session

1. _____
   _____
2. _____
   _____
3. _____
   _____

Discoveries or Learnings for This Session

1. _____
   _____
2. _____
   _____
3. _____
   _____

_____

Points to Sharpen:

_____

Things to Remember:

Be willing to be a beginner every single morning.
— Meister Eckhart

Mount

Side Mount

Guard

Half Guard

Back

Standing

Date: ___/___/____

Technique: _____

Instructor: _____

Attack

Defend

Indicators/Start Point:

_____

Description of Technique:

_____

Critical Details:

Gi

No Gi

Both

# of Practices _____

PRACTICE NOTES

Goals for This Session

1. _____
   _____

2. _____
   _____

3. _____
   _____

Discoveries or Learnings for This Session

1. _____
   _____

2. _____
   _____

3. _____
   _____

Points to Sharpen:

Things to Remember:

This may be the hardest lesson of all: that pain and adversity are not a challenge, but an opportunity—a gift from the universe, a blessing from God. If you know what you're afraid to do, you know exactly what you should do next.
— Joe De Sena

Mount Side Mount Guard Half Guard Back Standing

Date: ___/___/____

Technique: _____

Instructor: _____

Attack ⟨

Defend ⟨

Indicators/Start Point:

_____

Description of Technique:

_____

Critical Details:

Gi ⟨

No Gi ⟨

Both ⟨

# of Practices _____

PRACTICE NOTES

Goals for This Session

1. _____
   _____
2. _____
   _____
3. _____
   _____

Discoveries or Learnings for This Session

1. _____
   _____
2. _____
   _____
3. _____
   _____

_____

Points to Sharpen:

_____

Things to Remember:

You will never be entirely comfortable. This is the truth behind the champion—he is always fighting something. To do otherwise is to settle.
— Julien Smith

Mount

Side Mount

Guard

Half Guard

Back

Standing

Date: ___/___/____

Technique: _____

Instructor: _____

Attack

Defend

Indicators/Start Point:

_____

Description of Technique:

_____

Critical Details:

Gi

No Gi

Both

# of Practices _____

PRACTICE NOTES

Goals for This Session

1. _____
   _____

2. _____
   _____

3. _____
   _____

Discoveries or Learnings for This Session

1. _____
   _____

2. _____
   _____

3. _____
   _____

_____

Points to Sharpen:

_____

Things to Remember:

It's not whether you get knocked down, it's whether you get up.
— Vince Lombardi

Mount

Side Mount

Guard

Half Guard

Back

Standing

Date: ___/___/____

Technique: _____

Instructor: _____

Attack

Defend

Indicators/Start Point:

_____

Description of Technique:

_____

Critical Details:

Gi

No Gi

Both

# of Practices _____

PRACTICE NOTES

Goals for This Session

1. _____
   _____
2. _____
   _____
3. _____
   _____

Discoveries or Learnings for This Session

1. _____
   _____
2. _____
   _____
3. _____
   _____

Points to Sharpen:

Things to Remember:

Strategy without tactics is the slowest route to victory.
Tactics without strategy is the noise before defeat.
— Sun Tzu

Mount | Side Mount | Guard | Half Guard | Back | Standing

Date: ___/___/____

Technique: _____

Instructor: _____

Attack

Defend

Indicators/Start Point:

_____

Description of Technique:

_____

Critical Details:

Gi

No Gi

Both

# of Practices _____

PRACTICE NOTES

Goals for This Session

1. _____
   _____

2. _____
   _____

3. _____
   _____

Discoveries or Learnings for This Session

1. _____
   _____

2. _____
   _____

3. _____
   _____

Points to Sharpen:

Things to Remember:

Victory is always possible for the person who refuses to stop fighting.
— Napoleon Hill

Mount Side Mount Guard Half Guard Back Standing

Date: ___/___/____

Technique: _____

Instructor: _____

Attack ⟨

Defend ⟨

Indicators/Start Point:

_____

Description of Technique:

_____

Critical Details:

Gi ⟨

No Gi ⟨

Both ⟨

# of Practices _____

PRACTICE NOTES

Goals for This Session

1. _____
   _____
2. _____
   _____
3. _____
   _____

Discoveries or Learnings for This Session

1. _____
   _____
2. _____
   _____
3. _____
   _____

Points to Sharpen:

Things to Remember:

However beautiful the strategy, you should occasionally look at the results.
— Sir Winston Churchill

Mount

Side Mount

Guard

Half Guard

Back

Standing

Date: ___/___/____

Technique: _____

Instructor: _____

Attack 〈

Defend 〈

Indicators/Start Point:

_____

Description of Technique:

_____

Critical Details:

Gi 〈

No Gi 〈

Both 〈

# of Practices _____

PRACTICE NOTES

Goals for This Session

1. _____
   _____

2. _____
   _____

3. _____
   _____

Discoveries or Learnings for This Session

1. _____
   _____

2. _____
   _____

3. _____
   _____

_____

Points to Sharpen:

_____

Things to Remember:

Good judgement is the result of experience,
and experience the result of bad judgement.
— Mark Twain

Mount

Side Mount

Guard

Half Guard

Back

Standing

Date: ___/___/____

Technique: _____

Instructor: _____

Attack ⟨

Defend ⟨

Indicators/Start Point:

_____

Description of Technique:

_____

Critical Details:

Gi ⟨

No Gi ⟨

Both ⟨

# of Practices _____

PRACTICE NOTES

Goals for This Session

1. _____
   _____
2. _____
   _____
3. _____
   _____

Discoveries or Learnings for This Session

1. _____
   _____
2. _____
   _____
3. _____
   _____

_____

Points to Sharpen:

_____

Things to Remember:

In the struggle between the stone and water, in time, the water wins.
— Japanese Proverb

Mount

Side Mount

Guard

Half Guard

Back

Standing

Date: ___/___/____

Technique: _____

Instructor: _____

Attack

Defend

Indicators/Start Point:

_____

Description of Technique:

_____

Critical Details:

Gi

No Gi

Both

# of Practices _____

PRACTICE NOTES

Goals for This Session

1. _____
   _____

2. _____
   _____

3. _____
   _____

Discoveries or Learnings for This Session

1. _____
   _____

2. _____
   _____

3. _____
   _____

_____

Points to Sharpen:

_____

Things to Remember:

— The successful warrior is the average man, with laser-like focus.
— Bruce Lee

Mount   Side Mount   Guard   Half Guard   Back   Standing

Date: ___/___/____

Technique: _____

Instructor: _____

Attack

Defend

Indicators/Start Point:

_____

Description of Technique:

_____

Critical Details:

Gi

No Gi

Both

# of Practices _____

PRACTICE NOTES

Goals for This Session

1. _____
   _____
2. _____
   _____
3. _____
   _____

Discoveries or Learnings for This Session

1. _____
   _____
2. _____
   _____
3. _____
   _____

_____

Points to Sharpen:

_____

Things to Remember:

The tragedy of life lies not in not reaching your goals, but in having no goals to reach.
— Benjamin Elijah Mays

Mount Side Mount Guard Half Guard Back Standing

Date: ___/___/____

Technique: _____

Instructor: _____

Attack

Defend

Indicators/Start Point:

_____

Description of Technique:

_____

Critical Details:

Gi

No Gi

Both

# of Practices _____

PRACTICE NOTES

Goals for This Session

1. _____
_____

2. _____
_____

3. _____
_____

Discoveries or Learnings for This Session

1. _____
_____

2. _____
_____

3. _____
_____

Points to Sharpen:

Things to Remember:

Learning defense improves the attack. If the lion knows how
the prey can escape, it'll capture it in a much more precise way.
— Rillion Gracie

Mount

Side Mount

Guard

Half Guard

Back

Standing

Date: ___/___/____

Technique: _____

Instructor: _____

Attack

Defend

Indicators/Start Point:

_____

Description of Technique:

_____

Critical Details:

Gi

No Gi

Both

# of Practices _____

PRACTICE NOTES

Goals for This Session

1. _____
   _____

2. _____
   _____

3. _____
   _____

Discoveries or Learnings for This Session

1. _____
   _____

2. _____
   _____

3. _____
   _____

_____

Points to Sharpen:

_____

Things to Remember:

Only a fool does something new and thinks it will work for sure.
Only a failure refuses to try something that might not work.
— Seth Godin

Mount

Side Mount

Guard

Half Guard

Back

Standing

Date: ___/___/____

Technique: _____

Instructor: _____

Attack ⟨

Defend ⟨

Indicators/Start Point:

_____

Description of Technique:

_____

Critical Details:

Gi ⟨

No Gi ⟨

Both ⟨

# of Practices _____

PRACTICE NOTES

Goals for This Session

1. _____
   _____
2. _____
   _____
3. _____
   _____

Discoveries or Learnings for This Session

1. _____
   _____
2. _____
   _____
3. _____
   _____

_____

Points to Sharpen:

_____

Things to Remember:

Knowing is not enough; we must apply. Willing is not enough; we must do.
— Johann Wolfgang von Goethe

Mount
Side Mount
Guard
Half Guard
Back
Standing

Date: ___/___/____

Technique: _____

Instructor: _____

Attack

Defend

Indicators/Start Point:

_____

Description of Technique:

_____

Critical Details:

Gi

No Gi

Both

# of Practices _____

PRACTICE NOTES

Goals for This Session

1. _____
   _____
2. _____
   _____
3. _____
   _____

Discoveries or Learnings for This Session

1. _____
   _____
2. _____
   _____
3. _____
   _____

_____

Points to Sharpen:

_____

Things to Remember:

Always do your best. What you plant now, you will harvest later.
— Og Mandino

Mount | Side Mount | Guard | Half Guard | Back | Standing

Date: ___/___/____

Technique: _____

Instructor: _____

Attack ⟨

Defend ⟨

Indicators/Start Point:

_____

Description of Technique:

_____

Critical Details:

Gi ⟨

No Gi ⟨

Both ⟨

# of Practices _____

PRACTICE NOTES

Goals for This Session

1. _____
   _____
2. _____
   _____
3. _____
   _____

Discoveries or Learnings for This Session

1. _____
   _____
2. _____
   _____
3. _____
   _____

Points to Sharpen:

Things to Remember:

The opportunity of defeating the enemy is provided by the enemy himself.
— Sun Tzu

Mount

Side Mount

Guard

Half Guard

Back

Standing

Date: ___/___/____

Technique: _____

Instructor: _____

Attack

Defend

Indicators/Start Point:

_____

Description of Technique:

_____

Critical Details:

Gi

No Gi

Both

# of Practices _____

PRACTICE NOTES

Goals for This Session

1. _____
   _____
2. _____
   _____
3. _____
   _____

Discoveries or Learnings for This Session

1. _____
   _____
2. _____
   _____
3. _____
   _____

Points to Sharpen:

Things to Remember:

When you fail you learn from the mistakes you
made and it motivates you to work even harder.
— Natalie Gulbis

Mount

Side Mount

Guard

Half Guard

Back

Standing

Date: ___/___/____

Technique: _____

Instructor: _____

Attack

Defend

Indicators/Start Point:

_____

Description of Technique:

_____

Critical Details:

Gi

No Gi

Both

# of Practices _____

PRACTICE NOTES

Goals for This Session

1. _____
   _____
2. _____
   _____
3. _____
   _____

Discoveries or Learnings for This Session

1. _____
   _____
2. _____
   _____
3. _____
   _____

_____

Points to Sharpen:

_____

Things to Remember:

When the enemy is relaxed, make them toil. When
full, starve them. When settled, make them move.
— Sun Tzu

Mount

Side Mount

Guard

Half Guard

Back

Standing

Date: ___/___/____

Technique: _____

Instructor: _____

Attack (

Defend (

Indicators/Start Point:

_____

Description of Technique:

_____

Critical Details:

Gi (

No Gi (

Both (

# of Practices _____

PRACTICE NOTES

Goals for This Session

1. _____
   _____

2. _____
   _____

3. _____
   _____

Discoveries or Learnings for This Session

1. _____
   _____

2. _____
   _____

3. _____
   _____

_____

Points to Sharpen:

_____

Things to Remember:

The will to succeed is important, but what's more important is the will to prepare.
— Bobby Knight

Mount

Side Mount

Guard

Half Guard

Back

Standing

Date: ___/___/____

Technique: _____

Instructor: _____

Attack

Defend

Indicators/Start Point:

_____

Description of Technique:

_____

Critical Details:

Gi

No Gi

Both

# of Practices _____

PRACTICE NOTES

Goals for This Session

1. _____
   _____
2. _____
   _____
3. _____
   _____

Discoveries or Learnings for This Session

1. _____
   _____
2. _____
   _____
3. _____
   _____

_____

Points to Sharpen:

_____

Things to Remember:

Step by step and the thing is done.
— Charles Atlas

Mount

Side Mount

Guard

Half Guard

Back

Standing

Date: ___/___/____

Technique: _____

Instructor: _____

Attack

Defend

Indicators/Start Point:

_____

Description of Technique:

_____

Critical Details:

Gi

No Gi

Both

# of Practices _____

PRACTICE NOTES

Goals for This Session

1. _____
   _____

2. _____
   _____

3. _____
   _____

Discoveries or Learnings for This Session

1. _____
   _____

2. _____
   _____

3. _____
   _____

_____

Points to Sharpen:

_____

Things to Remember:

What you get by achieving your goals is not as
important as what you become by achieving your goals.
— Zig Ziglar

Mount | Side Mount | Guard | Half Guard | Back | Standing

Date: ___/___/____

Technique: _____

Instructor: _____

Attack

Defend

Indicators/Start Point:

_____

Description of Technique:

_____

Critical Details:

Gi

No Gi

Both

# of Practices _____

PRACTICE NOTES

Goals for This Session

1. _____
   _____

2. _____
   _____

3. _____
   _____

Discoveries or Learnings for This Session

1. _____
   _____

2. _____
   _____

3. _____
   _____

_____

Points to Sharpen:

_____

Things to Remember:

The key is to keep company only with people who
uplift you, whose presence calls forth your best.
— Epictetus

Mount

Side Mount

Guard

Half Guard

Back

Standing

Date: ___/___/____

Technique: _____

Instructor: _____

Attack ⟨

Defend ⟨

Indicators/Start Point:

_____

Description of Technique:

_____

Critical Details:

Gi ⟨

No Gi ⟨

Both ⟨

# of Practices _____

PRACTICE NOTES

Goals for This Session

1. _____
   _____

2. _____
   _____

3. _____
   _____

Discoveries or Learnings for This Session

1. _____
   _____

2. _____
   _____

3. _____
   _____

_____

Points to Sharpen:

_____

Things to Remember:

A creative man is motivated by the desire to achieve, not by the desire to beat others.
— Ayn Rand

Mount

Side Mount

Guard

Half Guard

Back

Standing

Date: ___/___/____

Technique: _____

Instructor: _____

Attack

Defend

Indicators/Start Point:

_____

Description of Technique:

_____

Critical Details:

Gi

No Gi

Both

# of Practices _____

PRACTICE NOTES

Goals for This Session

1. _____
   _____

2. _____
   _____

3. _____
   _____

Discoveries or Learnings for This Session

1. _____
   _____

2. _____
   _____

3. _____
   _____

_____

Points to Sharpen:

_____

Things to Remember:

Using order to deal with the disorderly, using calm
to deal with the clamorous, is mastering the heart.
— Sun Tzu

Mount

Side Mount

Guard

Half Guard

Back

Standing

Date: ___/___/____

Technique: _____

Instructor: _____

Attack

Defend

Indicators/Start Point:

_____

Description of Technique:

_____

Critical Details:

Gi

No Gi

Both

# of Practices _____

PRACTICE NOTES

Goals for This Session

1. _____
   _____
2. _____
   _____
3. _____
   _____

Discoveries or Learnings for This Session

1. _____
   _____
2. _____
   _____
3. _____
   _____

Points to Sharpen:

Things to Remember:

It's always too early to quit.
— Norman Vincent Peale

Mount

Side Mount

Guard

Half Guard

Back

Standing

Date: ___/___/____

Technique: _____

Instructor: _____

Attack

Defend

Indicators/Start Point:

_____

Description of Technique:

_____

Critical Details:

Gi

No Gi

Both

# of Practices _____